j
599
Har
c.2

ENDANGERED AND THREATENED ANIMALS

THE ORANGUTAN

A MyReportLinks.com Book

Lisa Harkrader

MyReportLinks.com Books
an imprint of
Enslow Publishers, Inc.
Box 398, 40 Industrial Road
Berkeley Heights, NJ 07922
USA

MyReportLinks.com Books, an imprint of Enslow Publishers, Inc. MyReportLinks® is a registered trademark of Enslow Publishers, Inc.

Copyright © 2005 by Enslow Publishers, Inc.

All rights reserved.

No part of this book may be reproduced by any means without the written permission of the publisher.

Library of Congress Cataloging-in-Publication Data

Harkrader, Lisa.
  The orangutan / Lisa Harkrader.
    p. cm. — (Endangered and threatened animals)
  Includes bibliographical references and index.
  ISBN 0-7660-5068-8
  1. Orangutan—Juvenile literature. I. Title. II. Series.
  QL737.P96H365 2005
  599.88'3—dc22
                                    2004027578

Printed in the United States of America

10 9 8 7 6 5 4 3 2 1

To Our Readers:
Through the purchase of this book, you and your library gain access to the Report Links that specifically back up this book.
The Publisher will provide access to the Report Links that back up this book and will keep these Report Links up to date on **www.myreportlinks.com** for five years from the book's first publication date.
We have done our best to make sure all Internet addresses in this book were active and appropriate when we went to press. However, the author and the Publisher have no control over, and assume no liability for, the material available on those Internet sites or on other Web sites they may link to. The usage of the MyReportLinks.com Books Web site is subject to the terms and conditions stated on the Usage Policy Statement on **www.myreportlinks.com**.
A password may be required to access the Report Links that back up this book. The password is found on the bottom of page 4 of this book.
Any comments or suggestions can be sent by e-mail to comments@myreportlinks.com or to the address on the back cover.

Photo Credits: © 1997, 1996 T/Maker Company, p. 10; © Brand X Pictures, p. 25; © Corel Corporation, pp. 1, 3, 18, 27, 28, 38, 44; Borneo Orangutan Survival Foundation, p. 40; BOS-USA, p. 33; Enslow Publishers, Inc., p. 13; Honolulu Zoo, pp. 17, 42; John Bavaro, p. 15; MyReportLinks.com Books, p. 4; Orangutan Foundation International, p. 36; Photos.com, p. 22; Science News for Kids, p. 30; Wally Santana/AP/Wide World Photos, p. 34.

Cover Photo: © Brand X Pictures.

Contents

	Report Links	4
	Orangutan Facts	10
1	The Endangered Orangutan	11
2	Orangutan Characteristics	15
3	Life in the Treetops	21
4	Orangutan Intelligence	26
5	Saving the Orangutan	32
	The Endangered and Threatened Wildlife List	45
	Chapter Notes	46
	Further Reading	47
	Index	48

About MyReportLinks.com Books

MyReportLinks.com Books
Great Books, Great Links, Great for Research!

The Internet sites listed on the next five pages can save you hours of research time. These Internet sites—we call them "Report Links"—are constantly changing, but we keep them up to date on our Web site.

Give it a try! Type http://www.myreportlinks.com into your browser, click on the series title, then the book title, and scroll down to the Report Links listed for this book.

The Report Links will bring you to great source documents, photographs, and illustrations. MyReportLinks.com Books save you time, feature Report Links that are kept up to date, and make report writing easier than ever!

Please see "To Our Readers" on the copyright page for important information about this book, the MyReportLinks.com Web site, and the Report Links that back up this book.

Please enter **EOR1423** if asked for a password.

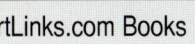

Tools   Search   Notes   Discuss

Report Links

 The Internet sites described below can be accessed at
http://www.myreportlinks.com

*Editor's choice

▶ **Animal Bytes: Orangutan**
Learning about the orangutan is fun when you visit this San Diego Zoo Web site. Besides great information and fun facts, there is a video to watch and sound files to listen to of the park's orangutans.

Link to this Internet site from http://www.myreportlinks.com

*Editor's choice

▶ **Great Apes & Other Primates: Orangutans**
Read about orangutans on this Smithsonian site that also has links to sites about other primates. Intelligence and a well-adapted body help orangutans survive in the tropical rain forests of Sumatra and Borneo.

Link to this Internet site from http://www.myreportlinks.com

*Editor's choice

▶ **Sumatran Orangutan Society**
The Sumatran orangutan is a critically endangered species. The Sumatran Orangutan Society is dedicated to preserving and protecting this great ape. Learn more about Sumatran orangutans from this site.

Link to this Internet site from http://www.myreportlinks.com

*Editor's choice

▶ **Orangutan Foundation International**
The Orangutan Foundation International is one of the leading nonprofit organizations dedicated to the survival of orangutans. The group's Web site contains orangutan facts and figures, photographs, and sound files.

Link to this Internet site from http://www.myreportlinks.com

*Editor's choice

▶ **Meet the "Red People of the Forest"**
This World Wildlife Federation Web page on the orangutan offers a wealth of information on orangutans and the other great apes.

Link to this Internet site from http://www.myreportlinks.com

*Editor's choice

▶ **Orangutans: Just Hangin' On**
Orangutans are highly intelligent animals that can skillfully use tools such as leaves for umbrellas and cups as well as sticks for opening prickly fruit. This PBS site looks into orangutan intelligence, tool use, and the campaign to save the animal from extinction.

Link to this Internet site from http://www.myreportlinks.com

Any comments? Contact us: comments@myreportlinks.com   5

Report Links

The Internet sites described below can be accessed at
http://www.myreportlinks.com

▶ **Absolutely Apes**
Get a glimpse of the apes from the San Diego Zoo without leaving your computer. On this zoo site, see if you can spot any of these creatures on the zoo's "Ape Cam." A description of the zoo's animals is included.

Link to this Internet site from http://www.myreportlinks.com

▶ **All About Orangutans**
The orangutan is only found in the wild rain forests of Borneo and Sumatra. Next to the gorilla, it is the largest primate. Find out more about the animal on this site.

Link to this Internet site from http://www.myreportlinks.com

▶ **Biruté Galdikas**
Dr. Biruté Galdikas, considered the foremost expert on orangutans, has been studying these great apes in the wild since the early 1970s. Read a brief biography of Dr. Galdikas on this site.

Link to this Internet site from http://www.myreportlinks.com

▶ **Blocking the Road to Extinction**
With the lowest reproduction rates of all mammals and a rapidly disappearing habitat, orangutans are vulnerable to extinction. Learn more about research on orangutans at this Harvard University Web site.

Link to this Internet site from http://www.myreportlinks.com

▶ **Borneo Forest Faces Extinction**
Borneo was once known as the lungs of Asia because of its huge rain forest. Currently, 60 percent of its protected national parkland is illegally logged, and many rain-forest animals are starving and in decline. This *Wired* article provides details.

Link to this Internet site from http://www.myreportlinks.com

▶ **The Borneo Orangutan Survival Foundation (BOS)**
A large number of Bornean orangutans have been lost due to the effects of logging, hunting, poaching, and the fires of 1997. Find out how this organization is trying to save the Bornean orangutan and reintroduce the animal into the wild.

Link to this Internet site from http://www.myreportlinks.com

Any comments? Contact us: **comments@myreportlinks.com**

Tools Search Notes Discuss MyReportLinks.com Books Go!

Report Links

 The Internet sites described below can be accessed at http://www.myreportlinks.com

▶ **BOS-USA**
From this site, learn about the orangutan, the animal that shares much of the same DNA as humans. Information on its habitat, diet, intelligence, and daily activities is included.

Link to this Internet site from http://www.myreportlinks.com

▶ **Camp Leakey**
Established in 1971 in the Tanjung Puting Reserve in Borneo, Camp Leakey provides a place for scientists to research orangutans and other animals in their natural habitat. Read about this facility, and view images of its different areas on this site.

Link to this Internet site from http://www.myreportlinks.com

▶ **Honolulu Zoo: Orangutan**
Learn about orangutan history and behavior from this site. Information on reproduction, conservation, and threats to survival is also available, including a section on the illegal pet trade and orangutan orphans.

Link to this Internet site from http://www.myreportlinks.com

▶ **The Introspective Orangutan**
Scientists working with orangutans report that these great apes exhibit high levels of intelligence and distinct personality traits, such as jealousy and patience. Two videos of orangutans are also included on this Web site.

Link to this Internet site from http://www.myreportlinks.com

▶ **The Leakey Foundation**
A leader in orangutan research, the Leakey Foundation is a supporter of long-term orangutan studies. From its site, learn about its research focusing on orangutan behavior, socialization, communication, and culture, which helps us better understand human evolution.

Link to this Internet site from http://www.myreportlinks.com

▶ **Meet the Orangutans**
A number of orangutans call the National Zoo in Washington, D.C., home. Read about a few of them to find out what they eat and how they spend their time. Click on the "Think Tank Facility" link for additional information.

Link to this Internet site from http://www.myreportlinks.com

Any comments? Contact us: comments@myreportlinks.com

| Back | Forward | Stop | Review | Home | Explore | Favorites | History |

Report Links

 The Internet sites described below can be accessed at
http://www.myreportlinks.com

▶ Orangutan Foundation
The orangutan, the largest tree-dwelling mammal in the world, is found only in Borneo and Sumatra in Southeast Asia. This site provides information on orangutans and what is being done to try to save them from becoming extinct.

Link to this Internet site from http://www.myreportlinks.com

▶ The Orangutan Sanctuary
This York University Web site provides articles on orangutans, information and maps on orangutan rehabilitation sites, and data on distribution and threats to survival. It also includes photos and an extensive bibliography for further reading.

Link to this Internet site from http://www.myreportlinks.com

▶ Orangutan, *Pongo Pygmaeus*
This Colorado University Web site provides a good overview of orangutans. Information on the species' taxonomy, distribution, habitat, behavior, ecology, diet, reproduction, conservation status, and more is provided.

Link to this Internet site from http://www.myreportlinks.com

▶ Orangutans
This Harvard University site offers a great deal of research on orangutans, including information on the animals' environment, range, activity patterns, diet, social system, life cycle, cognition level, and status.

Link to this Internet site from http://www.myreportlinks.com

▶ The Orangutans of Ketambe
The Zoo Atlanta Web site offers a look at the zoo's Sumatran orangutans. Learn about the zoo's rehabilitation efforts on behalf of orangutans rescued from the illegal pet trade.

Link to this Internet site from http://www.myreportlinks.com

▶ Orangutans Show Signs of Culturally Based Traits
This Duke University article reports on findings that show orangutans enjoy a unique culture, evidenced by at least twenty-four socially based behavior patterns. Tool use, bedtime rituals, and food-collection techniques are some of those identified as signs of culture.

Link to this Internet site from http://www.myreportlinks.com

Any comments? Contact us: **comments@myreportlinks.com**

Tools Search Notes Discuss MyReportLinks.com Books Go!

Report Links

 The Internet sites described below can be accessed at
http://www.myreportlinks.com

▶ Primates in Peril
This Brookfield Zoo article takes a look at the threats that orangutans face in the wild and how the zoo's successful breeding program is one step in the preservation of the species. Tips on how you can make a difference are included.

Link to this Internet site from http://www.myreportlinks.com

▶ The Rainforest Alliance
The mission of the Rainforest Alliance is protecting rain forest ecosystems as well as the people and wildlife that depend on them. At the group's site, learn more about the rain forests where orangutans live and what is being done to save them.

Link to this Internet site from http://www.myreportlinks.com

▶ Species Information: Threatened and Endangered Animals and Plants
The United States Fish and Wildlife Service (FWS) lists threatened and endangered animals and plants worldwide. This FWS page offers links to the database in which those species, including the orangutan, are listed.

Link to this Internet site from http://www.myreportlinks.com

▶ Think Tank
The Think Tank at the National Zoo in Washington, D.C., gives scientists an opportunity to study the ways that orangutans, and other animals, use their intelligence. Read about this facility at the zoo's Web site.

Link to this Internet site from http://www.myreportlinks.com

▶ U.S. Supports Restricted Trade in Tropical Wood Ramin
This U.S. government article explains proposed regulations that would put greater restrictions on the international trade in ramin, a tropical hardwood tree that is logged illegally in Indonesia. The practice is one of the main causes for the depletion of orangutan habitats.

Link to this Internet site from http://www.myreportlinks.com

▶ Wild Orangutans: Extinct by 2023?
With more than 80 percent of orangutan habitat already destroyed, halting the pace of illegal logging is the key to saving the wild orangutan. Learn more about the animal's fight for survival from this *National Geographic* article.

Link to this Internet site from http://www.myreportlinks.com

Any comments? Contact us: **comments@myreportlinks.com**

Orangutan Facts

Scientific Name

Sumatran orangutans are *Pongo abelii*. Bornean orangutans are *Pongo pygmaeus*.

Height

Males average 4.5 feet (1.35 meters). Females average 3.5 feet (1.05 meters).

Weight

Males weigh from 165 to 300 pounds (75 to 136 kilograms) in the wild and up to 400 pounds (180 kilograms) or more in captivity. Females weigh from 80 to 120 pounds (36 to 54 kilograms).

Hair

Shaggy reddish brown to light orange. The hair of Bornean orangutans is smoother and browner. The hair of Sumatran orangutans is fluffier and redder.

Range

The rain forests of Borneo and Sumatra, two islands in Southeast Asia

Breeding Season

None. Orangutans, like humans, can breed at any time throughout the year, but females only mate and give birth every 7 to 9 years.

Gestation

8.5 months

Number of Young in One Birth

Usually only one young at birth

Life Span

They can live Up to 60 years in captivity

Status

Bornean orangutans are endangered. Sumatran orangutans are critically endangered.

Number of Individuals Remaining

Less than 50,000: approximately 30,000 to 40,000 in Borneo and 7,500 in Sumatra

Main Threat to Survival

Humans, who clear thousands of acres of rain forest each year for agriculture, logging, and mining

10

Chapter 1
The Endangered Orangutan

They are called "red apes," "people of the forest," and "wild men of Borneo." Because people pay more attention to African apes, such as gorillas and chimpanzees, they have been called "the neglected ape." Some native people of Borneo and Sumatra believed these apes were God's first try at making humans. Others thought they were humans who had fled to the forest. Native people believed these creatures knew how to talk but refused to speak in front of humans because they were afraid that humans would put them to work.

They are orangutans, the only great apes of Asia.

▶ A Shrinking Population

In ancient times, orangutans ranged through Southeast Asia into southern China and as far west as India. But at the end of the last ice age, ten thousand to twenty thousand years ago, orangutans disappeared on the mainland of Asia. Today they survive only in small pockets of rain forest on the islands of Sumatra and Borneo. Sumatra is part of the country of Indonesia. Borneo, the third largest island in the world after Greenland and Papua New Guinea, is divided into three countries. The southeastern two thirds of the island is part of Indonesia. The northern third is part of Malaysia. The tiny independent country of Brunei is notched out of the northwestern coast. Orangutans live in the Indonesian and Malaysian parts of Borneo.

Scientists estimate that in 1900, there were more than three hundred thousand orangutans living in the wild. Today, a little over one hundred years later, less than fifty thousand orangutans remain. Between thirty thousand and forty thousand live in Borneo, while about seventy-five hundred live in Sumatra.[1]

Bornean orangutans are listed as endangered, and Sumatran orangutans are critically endangered. Many countries give orangutans legal protection as endangered species. But their population has shrunk by half in the last ten years. The biggest threat to orangutans is the loss of their habitat. In the last three decades, nearly 100 million acres of Indonesia's rain forests have been cleared for logging, farming, and mining. Only 20 percent of the country's forests remain, and that number continues to shrink each year. Many scientists predict that without major conservation efforts, orangutans could become extinct within the next ten years.

▶ Illegal Pet Trade

In the 1980s, a popular television program called "The Naughty Family" aired in Taiwan. The show starred a family that owned a pet orangutan. Since then, many people in Asia have clamored to own pet orangutans, and although it is against the law to sell orangutans because they are endangered, an illegal orangutan trade has sprung up. Poachers kill mother orangutans and then take their babies to sell as pets on the black market. About two thirds of the captured babies die.

Researchers estimate that black marketers have sold more than two thousand baby orangutans as pets in the last few years. About twice that many—more than four thousand baby orangutans—died on their way to be

▲ *This map shows some of the orangutan wildlife refuges and rehabilitation centers in Indonesia and Malaysia.*

sold, and poachers shot six thousand mother orangutans to capture their babies. Ten thousand wild orangutans were killed so that two thousand babies could be shipped to Asia.

Those two thousand surviving babies have not fared well. Baby orangutans are cute and cuddly, but those babies grow up. Adult orangutans weigh as much as or more than adult humans and are much stronger. They are hard to manage, which leads some owners to just abandon them. Others take them to rehabilitation centers, where experts work toward one day releasing them into the wild.

▶ **Local Concerns**

Wild orangutans do not live in one country. Part of their habitat is in Indonesia, and part is in Malaysia. The borders between the countries make it hard to coordinate conservation efforts. The rain forest habitat is dense and

remote, which makes it difficult for governments to enforce conservation laws and keep orangutans and their habitat safe.

In recent years, the Indonesian government has been in a state of upheaval. In 1997, riots erupted throughout the country and forced the president to resign. In 1999, violence broke out in East Timor, a province that wanted to be independent from Indonesia. The political unrest has made orangutan protection even more difficult. And the horrible destruction and loss of life in coastal Sumatra caused by the earthquake and tsunami of December 2004 will only make it more difficult to save orangutans in a place where many people had little to begin with.

The poverty of this region is also one of the reasons that poaching goes on: Since those who sell endangered animals, like orangutans, are often poor, they can make more money in less time in illegal trade than they can earn honestly over a longer period. Most conservationists point out that it is too easy to simply blame native peoples for the reduction in animal populations in their countries. Those who provide the demand for the animals themselves as well as for the products that come from their habitats (such as tropical hardwoods) are at least as much to blame.

Finally, orangutans do not reproduce quickly. In fact, they reproduce slower than any other mammal. Female orangutans do not begin having babies until they are about twelve years old. They then give birth about every eight years and have only one baby at a time. A female orangutan will only have two to four babies in her lifetime. This slow reproduction rate means that when the orangutan population suffers a serious decline, it cannot bounce back quickly.

Chapter 2
Orangutan Characteristics

The orangutan's scientific name is *Pongo pygmaeus*, which means "short ape." Biologists classify the orangutans in Borneo and Sumatra as two separate species. Bornean orangutans are *Pongo pygmaeus*, and Sumatran orangutans are *Pongo abelii*.

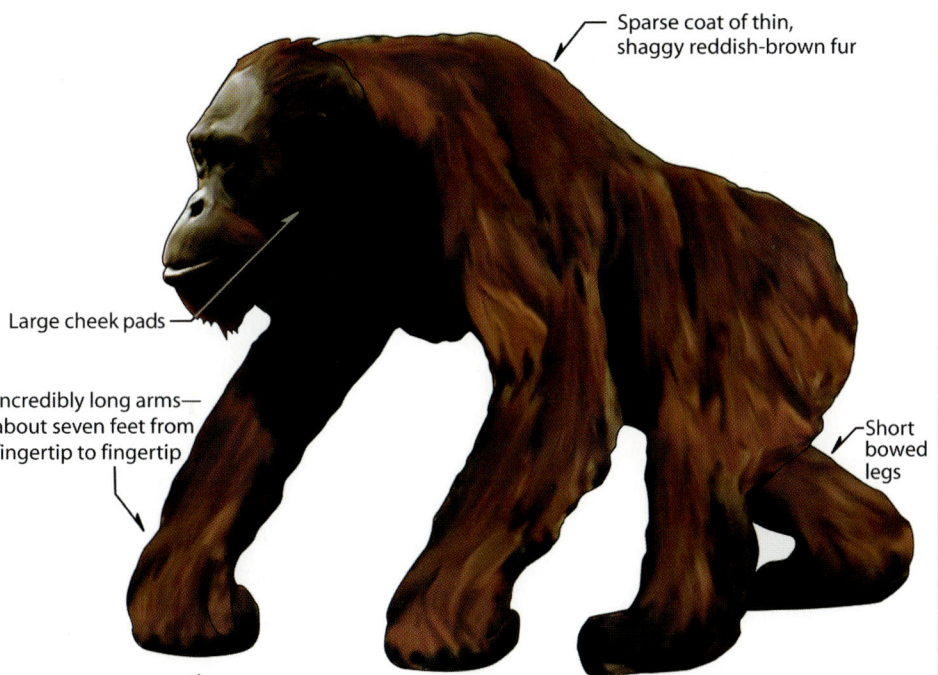

- Sparse coat of thin, shaggy reddish-brown fur
- Large cheek pads
- Incredibly long arms—about seven feet from fingertip to fingertip
- Short bowed legs
- Long, narrow hands and feet aid in grasping branches. Hands and feet like those of humans, with short opposable thumbs and big toes.

▲ Although orangutans can walk upright, like all great apes, they travel on all fours more often.

The people of Borneo and Sumatra speak Malay. The orangutan's common name comes from two Malay words: *orang,* which means "person," and *hutan,* which means "forest." Orangutan, then, means "person of the forest." It is considered inappropriate in Southeast Asia, however, to refer to orangutans by the shortened form "orang," because of the word's meaning.

▶ The Great Apes

Orangutans, gorillas, chimpanzees, and bonobos (once called pygmy chimpanzees) all belong to a group known as the great apes. Great apes are man's closest relatives. In fact, some scientists think humans should be classified as great apes. By studying fossils and DNA, or genetic material, scientists have determined that humans and apes evolved from a common ancestor that lived over 15 million years ago. Chimpanzees and bonobos are the most genetically similar to us. They share nearly 99 percent of their genes with humans, and humans can receive blood transfusions from chimpanzees. Humans and orangutans share 98 percent of their genes.[1]

But humans and orangutans share some characteristics that chimpanzees and gorillas do not share. Humans and orangutans have more parasites in common. They both have a certain vein in their arms that other apes do not have. All great apes can stand and walk upright, similar to the way that humans walk, but orangutans more often travel on all fours. When bonobos, chimpanzees, and gorillas travel on all fours, they "knuckle walk" by leaning on the knuckles of their hands. By contrast, orangutans ball their fingers into fists when they walk on all fours.

▶ The Treetop Ape

Orangutans are covered with reddish-brown hair, which gives them the nickname "red apes." They have short legs and long arms that span 7 to 8 feet (2.1 to 2.4 meters) from fingertip to fingertip in the largest males. Their arms are almost as long as the length of their bodies and legs put together.

Orangutans are the world's largest arboreal, or tree-dwelling, animals, and their bodies are well suited to their treetop habitat. Their long fingers wrap around vines and branches in a powerful, hooklike grip. Their thumbs are

▲ *Rusti, a male orangutan, is seen in his temporary headquarters at the Honolulu Zoo. A new home is being built for him there, complete with trees to swing from, rather than the makeshift "branches" pictured here.*

located low on their hands, far below their fingers. This helps keep an orangutan's thumbs out of the way when the animal brachiates, or moves hand over hand, as it travels from branch to branch.

Orangutans' handlike feet and rotating hip joints make them seem to have four arms instead of two arms and two legs. Any one of their limbs is strong enough to support their weight, so that they can hang by one hand or one foot without falling. Their long arms and agile legs also help them reach fruit and other food. They can even eat with their feet!

Males and Females

Adult male orangutans are so different in appearance from adult female orangutans that it is easy to tell them apart just by looking at them. Because of these differences, scientists once considered them to be two separate species.

Wild adult male orangutans are 4 to 5 feet (1.2 to 1.5 meters) tall and

◀ Adult female orangutans are about half as big as their male counterparts.

weigh from 165 pounds to a hefty 300 pounds (75 to 136 kilograms). Female orangutans are about half that size. Adult females average 3.5 feet (1.05 meters) in height and weigh from 80 to 120 pounds (36 to 54 kilograms).

But the size difference is not the only thing that sets males and females apart. When males reach maturity, at about age fifteen, they develop huge cheek pads that flare from the sides of their faces. These cheek pads make them look bigger and help them attract females. It is also believed that the cheek pads help the male's booming call travel farther in the forest, to reach other orangutans in the widely spaced community. When male orangutans fight, they often bite each other's cheek pads.

Mature males also develop a large throat pouch. The pouch is an air sac that hangs down below the orangutan's chin. The male uses his throat pouch to make his "long call," a series of throaty grunts and roars that can be heard for over half a mile. The long call attracts females and also helps the male compete with other males.

▶ Two Species?

For many years, biologists divided orangutans into two subspecies. Orangutans that live in Borneo were known as *Pongo pygmaeus pygmaeus*. Orangutans from Sumatra were *Pongo pygmaeus abelii*.

Bornean orangutans and Sumatran orangutans look very similar, although they do have a few differences. Sumatran orangutans have longer, fluffier, redder hair. Bornean orangutans' hair tends to be thicker, smoother, darker, and browner. Bornean orangutans also have wider faces, and the cheek pads of Bornean males grow forward, giving them a concave, or dish-faced, look.

In the 1980s, some scientists began questioning whether Sumatran and Bornean orangutans were more than subspecies. They believed the two groups could be separate species altogether. Borneo's orangutans live in five isolated populations, some separated by mountain ranges. Researchers wondered if these populations were different enough to be considered separate subspecies.

In the 1990s, a team of scientists led by Dr. Stephen J. O'Brien compared the DNA of Sumatran and Bornean orangutans. They found that the two groups of orangutans are as genetically different from each other as lions are from tigers, or horses from donkeys. In the great ape family, the orangutans are as different from each other as common chimpanzees are from bonobos.[2] Chimpanzees and bonobos have long been recognized as separate species.

By studying the orangutans' DNA, Dr. O'Brien and his team determined that Sumatran and Bornean orangutans evolved from a common orangutan ancestor about one million to three million years ago.[3] They also discovered that the different populations of Bornean orangutans show very little genetic difference. They believe that until very recently, these populations were not as separate as they are now. The populations only became isolated from each other within the last century, as humans began clearing large areas of rain forest.[4]

Chapter 3 ▶

Life in the Treetops

Orangutans are difficult to study in the wild. In fact, they are difficult to find at all, since orangutans live high in the forest canopy, often 100 feet (30.5 meters) or more from the ground. They are quiet, slow-moving apes that blend in with their surroundings. Some orangutans, especially those in Sumatra, live in rain forest so dense and swampy that researchers find it difficult to even enter it to study the apes.

▶ Tree Dwellers

Orangutans do not move quickly, but they are experts at traveling among branches and vines. Wild female orangutans rarely set foot on the ground, even to find food or water. Adult males, though, do spend a fair amount of time on the ground, since they are usually too heavy to stay in the narrow tree branches. They eat fruits, plants, and animals they can find or catch in the trees. They drink rainwater that collects in the leaves and hollows of trees.

Orangutans are capable of walking. They sometimes walk on two feet, as humans do. But like other great apes, orangutans more often walk on all fours. They do not have the tough pads on their knuckles that gorillas and chimpanzees have. Instead, orangutans walk on the sides of their cupped hands and feet. Their walk looks a little awkward. Orangutans are much more confident and graceful when climbing and swinging through the trees.

◀ *The trees of the Sumatran and Bornean rain forests are home to orangutans.*

▶ Loners

Adult orangutans are usually described as solitary apes, although they demonstrate the same levels of social abilities as the African apes. Adult male orangutans certainly are loners. They live alone and will not tolerate other adult males in their territory. They seek out female orangutans when it is time to mate. They stay with a female only for a short time and then move on. In Sumatra, male orangutans sometimes stay with females until the female gives birth. Scientists believe that Sumatran males may stay longer to protect the female from Sumatran tigers. Tigers do not live in Borneo.

Adult female orangutans are seldom alone. They do not live in the company of other adult orangutans, but they are almost always raising young. Female orangutans give birth to their first baby when they are about twelve years old. They raise the baby for eight or nine years. The young orangutan often stays close to its mother for the next two or three years as the female gives birth again and begins raising her next infant.

Although orangutans are semisolitary, they are also adaptable. In places where fruit is ripe and plentiful, several female orangutans will feed together in the same tree. In some swampy, remote areas of rain forest, orangutans live closer together and are more social. Many orangutans, when freed from the constraints of their habitats, show a preference for social interaction with other orangutans.

Home on the Range

Adult orangutans establish home ranges. These are areas of the rain forest the orangutan travels through, gathering food. An orangutan's home range is not rigidly defined. Orangutans will venture beyond their usual ranges to find food. An orangutan's home range can stretch out over three square miles (eight square kilometers). In areas of rain forest where fruit and other food is abundant, ranges are smaller. In areas where food is scarce, ranges must be larger. A range must contain enough food to keep the orangutan alive.

Fruit Lovers

Orangutans are omnivores, eating both plants and animals. They eat leaves, nuts, shoots, honey, insects, and occasionally small birds and animals. In fact, the orangutan's diet is one of the most varied in the animal kingdom. Orangutans eat over four hundred different kinds of food.

But orangutans are also called frugivores, or fruit eaters, because their favorite food, by far, is fruit. They love some of the same fruits we enjoy, such as figs and mangoes. One of their favorite fruits is durian, a pungent fruit with a firm, prickly covering. The durian is popular with many animals in the rain forest, but its skin is so hard that other animals cannot eat it until the fruit is so ripe it bursts open. The strong and nimble-fingered orangutans, however, use their mouths and hands to open the fruit. Orangutans feast on durian long before other rain forest animals are able to.

Orangutans are diurnal—active and awake during the day. Each night, adult orangutans build a nest of branches and leaves to sleep in, rarely using a nest more than once. They build the nests in trees, 15 to 100 feet (4.6 to 30.5 meters) above the ground. Babies and young orangutans sleep in their mothers' nests.

▶ Mothers and Babies

Female orangutans give birth for the first time when they are about twelve years old. They are pregnant for about eight and a half months and usually give birth to one baby at a time.

Orangutan mothers give their new babies constant attention. For the first year, the orangutan mother carries her infant on her body all the time. The baby clings to its mother's hair and skin as she climbs through the forest.

At about age one, young orangutans become more independent. They stay very close to their mothers, but they no longer seem glued to her body. Their mothers teach them to climb, and the babies begin exploring and learning to navigate branches and trees on their own.

Orangutans have a longer childhood than any other animal except humans. Young orangutans have a lot to learn—and only one teacher. Their mothers teach them everything they need to know to survive in the rain forest. Mothers teach their young orangutans where to find the four hundred kinds of food that orangutans eat. At first, the mother orangutan feeds her baby bits of food she has already chewed. As the young orangutan grows, it

▲ *At about age one, young orangutans develop some independence but will still stay with their mothers for at least five more years.*

begins gathering food on its own. Mothers also teach their babies how to find and open fruit when it is ripe and how to build nests and stay out of danger.

By the time an orangutan is six years old, she has begun venturing farther from her mother. No longer sleeping with her mother, she builds her own sleeping nest nearby. The mother orangutan will have her next baby when her first child is seven or eight years old. At first, the older orangutan child may stay close to the mother and new baby, but eventually she will go off to establish her own home range. Males tend to leave their mothers earlier and travel far away to establish their home ranges. Females stay with their mothers longer and establish ranges close by.

Chapter 4 ▶

Orangutan Intelligence

It is difficult to measure the brainpower of animal species because different species show intelligence in different ways. They have different skills, depending on what their species needs to survive. But if intelligence is understood as the ability to adapt to changing circumstances and solve problems with creativity and imagination, nearly all scientists agree that great apes are some of the most intelligent animals in the world.

▶ Species Differences

Orangutans move slowly and deliberately. They often act as if they are not paying attention. For these reasons, people used to think that orangutans were the least intelligent of the great apes.

But researchers have found that orangutans are just as bright as other great apes. In fact, orangutans do better than gorillas and chimpanzees on some intelligence tests. This is because different ape species solve problems differently. When chimpanzees face a problem, such as trying to get food out of a closed box, they tend to dive in, actively and noisily. They first try one thing, then another. If they do not succeed within a few minutes, they may give up in frustration.

Jumping at a problem with great energy and activity but a short attention span is not an effective way to tackle problems in the rain forest. That is probably why orangutans tend to be more deliberate problem solvers. They may look as if they are not really paying attention, but they are, in fact, constantly watching their environment very closely. They usually do not look at things head-on but from the corners of their eyes. Researchers think that orangutans ponder a problem and possible solutions to it before they act. When they finally go toward the box of food, they often approach it with a very specific plan for opening it. And they work through their plan, step by step, until it succeeds.

Tools

One way in which scientists measure the intelligence of an animal species is by its use of tools. Species that use simple tools, such as sticks or rocks, are considered more intelligent than species that do not. Species that make or modify their tools are considered the most intelligent of all.

All great ape species use tools. They use sticks to dig for food on the ground, such as termites. They use rocks to break open nuts and fruits. Orangutans also

Orangutans are extremely intelligent creatures. Even when it appears that they are resting, they are actually keeping a keen eye on everything in their environment.

▲ *Orangutans' intelligence can also be seen in their use of natural objects, such as sticks and leaves, as tools.*

use sticks to scratch their backs and leafy branches to swat away insects. They use large leaves as natural umbrellas to shelter them from the sun and rain.

Orangutans also make or modify their tools. They chew leaves so that the leaves will act as sponges, absorbing water from tree hollows. The orangutans then suck the water from the leaves. When vines are too thin for an orangutan to travel on, orangutans can tie two vines together to increase their strength.

Orangutans are clever at imitating human behavior and learning to use human tools. Orangutans that have observed humans using boats to cross rivers have then untied the boats and set off across the water themselves. Captive orangutans have earned a reputation as escape artists. They continually find new ways to escape from their enclosures, such as by using a screwdriver to take apart a door's hinges. A large male orangutan named Fu Manchu kept escaping from his enclosure at the Omaha Zoo. The orangutan keepers finally discovered that Fu Manchu was using a piece of wire to pick the lock. During the day he would hide the wire in his mouth, between his lip and gum.[1]

Language

Great apes do not have the vocal structures that are required to produce human language, although they can produce sounds similar to ours. But they *do* have the ability to learn and use language. Researchers have taught great apes to communicate with humans through sign language. At the Think Tank's Orangutan Language Project at the Smithsonian Institution's National Zoo in Washington, D.C., orangutans learn to communicate by using special computers. The computers enable them to use about seventy different abstract symbols for words.

In the late 1970s, Dr. Gary Shapiro began teaching orangutans sign language at Camp Leakey, an orangutan research station in Borneo. At first, the orangutans did not seem to be interested in what he was showing them—they did not even seem to be paying attention at all. But when they began using the signs, Dr. Shapiro realized that they had been watching him all along.

Not only can orangutans (and other great apes) learn signs or symbols for different objects and actions, but they also use those signs correctly. They combine different signs into phrases, such as "give banana." They sometimes combine different signs to indicate a new object they do not already have a sign for. Chantek, a male orangutan at

▲ Like other great apes, orangutans have the ability to learn and use language. Chantek, a male at Zoo Atlanta, is able to use more than one hundred fifty signs to communicate with zoo officials.

Zoo Atlanta, knows over one hundred fifty signs. But he did not have a sign for Christmas, so he created his own: "Red Hat Day."²

▶ Culture

We think of *culture* as something that only describes humans. Groups of people who live in different parts of the world develop different cultures. The native people of Borneo, for example, developed social customs that were different from those of native Africans or Europeans.

But wildlife researchers are finding that individual populations of great ape species also develop different cultures, or sets of learned behaviors. The orangutans learn the behavior from each other and then pass it down from generation to generation. For example, orangutans often make a "kiss-squeak" noise when they are annoyed. But different orangutan populations make the kiss-squeak in different ways. Some Bornean populations kiss-squeak against a leaf to make the sound louder.

Orangutans in one Bornean population "snag ride." Snag riding is sort of an orangutan sport. The orangutan jumps onto a falling branch and rides it down through the rain forest. The orangutan catches itself on other branches or vines before the falling branch crashes to the rain forest floor. Orangutans in Sumatra as well as those in other Bornean populations do not snag ride, as far as researchers know.

One population of orangutans in Kutai National Park in eastern Borneo uses leaves as napkins. Some of the fruits they eat are particularly messy. They wipe the juice from their faces with leaf napkins. Even though other orangutan populations eat these same fruits, only the Kutai orangutans use leaves as napkins. A population of Sumatran orangutans on one side of a river uses sticks to open fruit and dig out the seeds. However, the population of orangutans on the other side of the river does not. Researchers have found that orangutans that live in the most social populations, such as those living in the dense, swampy rain forests in Sumatra, share the largest number of learned behaviors.

Chapter 5 ▶

Saving the Orangutan

Orangutans—those fascinating apes that seem so like us and at the same time, so different—are teetering on the brink of extinction.

The biggest threat to orangutans is loss of habitat. People continue to demolish over 6 million acres (2.4 million hectares) of Indonesian rain forest each year. In the past three decades, 99 million acres (40 million hectares) of Indonesia's forest—an area the size of Germany and the Netherlands combined—has been cut down. An estimated 16,000 acres (6,500 hectares) of Indonesian rain forest—an area the size of twelve football fields—is destroyed every minute.

Loss of habitat is also a critical problem in Malaysia. Environmentalists estimate that 190 acres (77 hectares) of Malaysian rain forest is felled every hour. The government of Malaysia continues to build large dams, such as the Bakun Dam in Borneo, which flood the surrounding land, destroying thousands of acres of rain forest.

But in this part of Southeast Asia, people as well as animals are having a tough time surviving. The Indian Ocean earthquake and tsunami of 2004 that destroyed significant parts of Sumatra and killed so many of its people has magnified that struggle. While orangutans were not affected by the destruction initially, the monumental task of rebuilding the Aceh province in northwestern Sumatra will almost certainly affect these great apes in the long term.

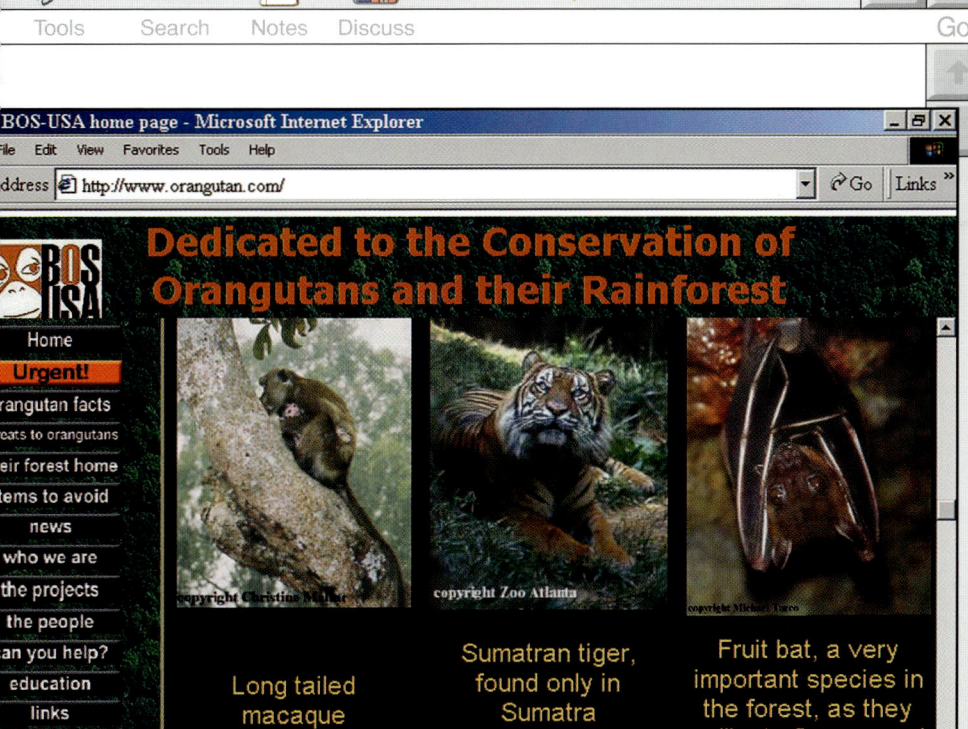

▲ The rain forests of Borneo and Sumatra, home to orangutans, are a fragile ecosystem where each species affects the other. Here, some of the forest's other animals are pictured.

Lori Perkins of Zoo Atlanta is the Orangutan Species Survival Plan (SSP) Coordinator and International Studbook Keeper for Orangutans. The SSP, administered by the American Zoo and Aquarium Association, is a cooperative breeding program to manage and conserve selected species in North American zoos. A studbook for each of these species contains vital records of an entire managed population. Ms. Perkins voiced the concerns of orangutan experts when asked about the effect of the tsunami on Sumatra's orangutans.

▲ A man from the Aceh province of northern Sumatra, who lost seven family members to the devastating tsunami of 2004, stands amid the rubble that was once his home.

The Leuser ecosystem, the only place where orangutans range in Sumatra, was largely untouched. However, the concern I've heard voiced is that as the human population begins to recover and starts rebuilding, they will need to use significant forest resources (timber) to do so, and that's when the tsunami will affect orangutans and other wildlife. Aceh has some of the largest forest areas left—and these areas are likely to be the easiest and least expensive source of timber for rebuilding as well. Whether the Indonesian government will opt to allow such use will remain to be seen—the focus is rightly on the human tragedy, but it's to be hoped that a wildlife tragedy won't result from addressing the human one.[1]

The key to saving the orangutan or any endangered species is to find a way for humans and animals to exist together without either population harming the other.

▶ Logging

Logging destroys much of the orangutan's habitat. The rain forests of Sumatra and Borneo are rich havens of tropical hardwood trees. The economies of Indonesia and Malaysia are poor, and the lumber from these trees is very valuable. Logging companies make a lot of money exporting lumber to other countries, and the industry creates much-needed jobs for local people. In addition, government officials often own the logging rights to areas of forest. These officials make money by leasing these rights to logging companies. So even though the rain forest is quickly disappearing, logging continues. Much of the logging is done illegally.

Logging companies also build roads through the rain forest, which destroys even more trees. The building of these roads erodes the soil and disrupts the natural balance of sunlight and humidity in the rain forest, putting plant and animals species that live there in peril. Roads also give poachers greater access into the dense rain forest, making it easier for them to kill mother orangutans and steal their babies. In addition, loggers hunt for most of their own food, depleting the forests of some of the orangutan's natural food sources. Sometimes they also hunt orangutans for food.

▶ Selective Logging

The Indonesian government tries to promote selective logging. In this method, rather than wiping out acres of rain forest at a time, loggers cut single trees here and there throughout the rain forest. Selective logging leaves the surrounding trees intact.

This sounds like a reasonable compromise. But rain forests are fragile and complicated ecosystems. The soil in a rain forest contains few nutrients. Most of the forest's nutrients lie in its towering trees. The tallest trees provide the most food and shelter for rain forest species. The tallest trees are the very trees that orangutans depend on for survival.

But the tallest trees are also the most valuable in the hardwood market. They are the trees that lumber companies target with selective logging. Even when loggers plant new trees to replace felled trees, the rain forest suffers permanent damage. In a natural cycle, when a tree dies, it

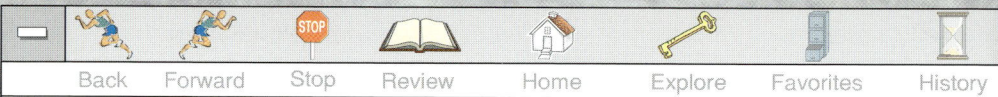

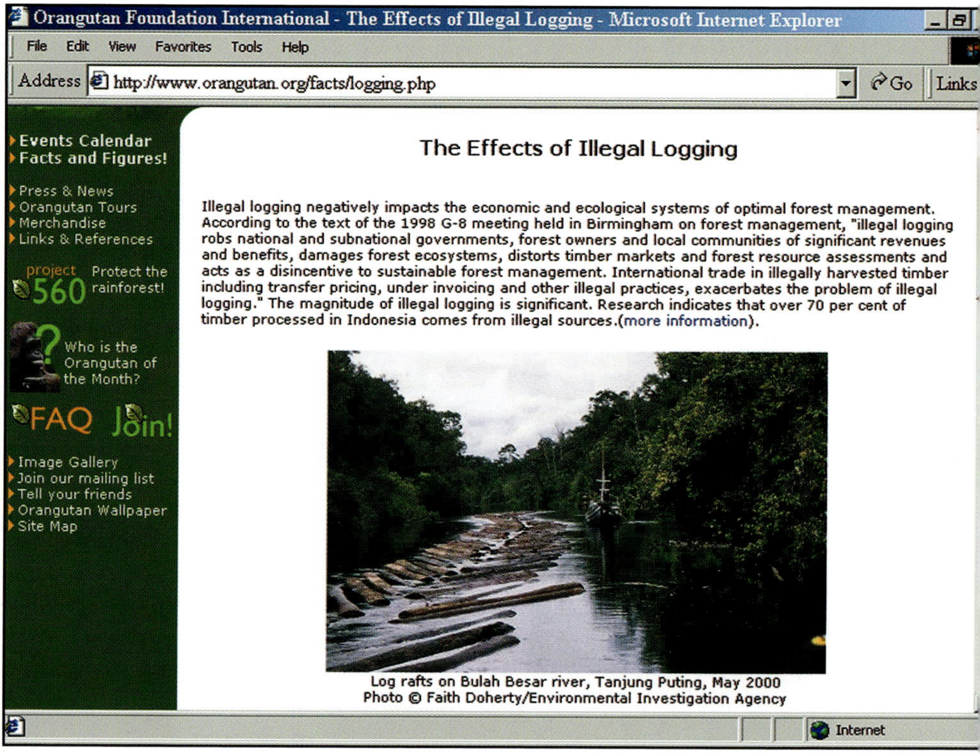

▲ It is thought that more than 70 percent of the timber produced in Indonesia comes from illegal sources. The destruction of the rain forests robs orangutans and other animals of their habitat.

falls to the floor of the rain forest. As the tree rots, its nutrients sink back into the soil and provide nourishment for young trees that spring up in its place. But when loggers remove a tree, its nutrients are gone forever. Nothing remains to nourish new trees. If loggers cut too many trees, the forest floor dries out, putting the entire forest at greater risk of fire. Orangutan populations in these logged forests have been seen to shrink by more than half.

▶ Plantations

Malaysia and Indonesia depend on palm oil to help their economies. Agricultural companies clear huge tracts of rain forest, up to 120 acres (49 hectares), for each palm plantation. To clear this land, plantation owners sometimes simply burn the forest down. In Borneo and Sumatra, almost all the lowland forests, the orangutan's favorite habitat, have been cleared. Orangutans have been forced into the higher forests, where food is not as plentiful. Fewer orangutans can survive in these higher forests.

Orangutans love to eat palm hearts, so they often invade plantations, foraging for food and damaging the palm trees. When plantation owners cannot scare them away or keep them out with fences, they often kill the trespassing orangutans. Some plantation owners put a bounty on orangutans. They pay local people up to a week's wages for each orangutan they kill.

▶ Mining

Gold mining has destroyed huge swaths of rain forest in Borneo. Miners use large water pumps and power hoses to blast away soil and dig holes into the earth. They leave behind nothing but craters in the barren sand. Miners also use heavy metals, such as mercury, to separate gold from sand. The mercury washes into the soil and runs into nearby streams and rivers, poisoning the land and water for the animals—and people—who depend on it to survive.

▶ Forest Fires

Over the last twenty years, forest fires have devastated Borneo and Sumatra. In 1983, the Great Fire of Borneo burned vast areas of rain forest. In 1991 and 1994, forest fires flared up again.

In 1997, immense fires erupted in Borneo. Fires in Sumatra and other nearby islands broke out as well. Scientists blamed the fires on a long drought caused by El Niño, a warm ocean current that delayed the annual monsoon rains. Logging made the forests even more vulnerable to fire. Loggers leave behind dried wood debris, as well as patches of grassland that grow up where the trees used to be, and these patches burn rapidly.

The fires raged for months and became the worst forest fire in history. Smoke choked the air and

◀ Orangutans have a taste for palm hearts, which sometimes puts them at odds with plantation owners whose palm trees have been damaged by the apes.

polluted the water. In the end, 25 percent of the rain forest in Borneo was destroyed.

▶ Working to Save Orangutans

The Convention on International Trade in Endangered Species of Wild Fauna and Flora (CITES) regulates international trade in endangered plants and animals. CITES lists orangutans in Appendix 1, its list of most-endangered species. The United States listed orangutans as an endangered species in 1970, offering the species additional regulations and protections. Many countries, including Malaysia, Indonesia, and Taiwan, have passed laws to protect orangutans. But these laws are hard to enforce against illegal loggers, miners, and poachers who sell orangutan babies as pets. Malaysia and Indonesia have established wildlife preserves and national parks. Rangers in these parks do their best to protect orangutans and other species, but it is often hard to guard the dense jungles.

Wildlife organizations around the world are fighting to save the orangutan. The Sumatran Orangutan Society, based in Bali but with branches in other countries, is on the front lines of the battle to save the critically endangered Sumatran orangutan. Orangutan Foundation International, the Borneo (or Balikpapan) Orangutan Survival Foundation, the World Wildlife Fund, and the Nature Conservancy help manage Bornean and Sumatran rain forests and help park rangers deal with illegal loggers and poachers. These groups try to protect orangutans that have overrun farms and plantations. They urge plantation owners to capture orangutans and take them to an orangutan rehabilitation center rather than killing them. They also try to educate people about the dangers that orangutans face and the ways in which humans can help them.

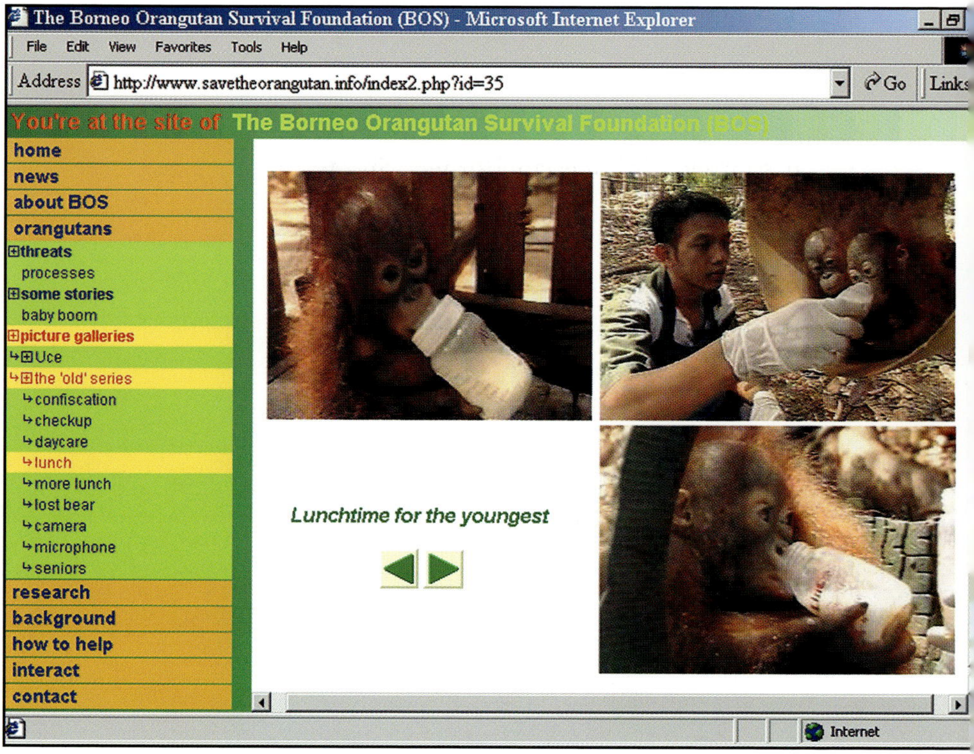

▲ Baby orangutans are cared for by workers at this rehabilitation center run by the Borneo Orangutan Survival Foundation.

Zoos have also played an important part in helping to save endangered orangutans and educate the public on the plight of these great apes, since orangutans generally do quite well in captivity. There are fifty-five zoological institutions in North America that participate in the Orangutan Species Survival Plan. The Orangutan SSP has led to the births of baby orangutans in captivity while the number of orangutans in the wild continues to drop. Zoo Atlanta, with eleven orangutans, has the largest population of orangutans in North America. There are about eight hundred orangutans in zoos worldwide.

Rehabilitation Centers

In 1971, Dr. Biruté Galdikas set up Camp Leakey in the Tanjung Puting Wildlife Reserve (now a national park) in southern Indonesian Borneo. She has studied orangutans at Camp Leakey for more than thirty years, was a cofounder of Orangutan Foundation International in 1986 (and is now its president), and is recognized as one of the world's leading experts on orangutans.

At Camp Leakey, Dr. Galdikas not only conducts research but also rehabilitates ex-captive and orphaned orangutans so that these great apes can be released back into the wild. Other orangutan rehabilitation centers include the Bohorok Orangutan Viewing Centre in Sumatra, the Wanariset Orangutan Rehabilitation and Reintroduction Center in Indonesian Borneo, and the Sepilok Orangutan Sanctuary in Malaysian Borneo.

When orangutans arrive at a rehab center, they live for a few weeks in quarantine, isolated from the other orangutans. During these weeks of quarantine, rehab workers can ensure that the new orangutan does not pass diseases on to the other orangutans. The workers can also treat sick or injured animals.

Once an ape is released from quarantine, rehab workers begin teaching it how to be a wild orangutan. Mother orangutans spend seven or eight years teaching their babies to survive in the rain forest. Orangutans that have been raised as pets have not learned those survival skills. Rehab centers try to teach these orangutans how to climb trees, find food, and build nests. It can take several years to teach an orangutan how to survive in the wild. When the orangutan is ready, rehab workers will release it into the wild. Once the orangutan is released, it can still return to the rehab center for feedings. Rehab workers hope that

▲ Dr. Biruté Galdikas, a cofounder of Orangutan Foundation International, has studied and worked with orangutans for more than thirty years.

a released orangutan will return to the center less and less over time until it finally becomes self-sufficient and no longer depends on the center for food.

Not all captive orangutans can become wild again, though. Some orangutans cannot learn the skills they need to survive because they have lived with people for too long and remain dependent on their human caregivers. These orangutans end up living in conservation centers for the rest of their lives. Expense is another concern. Rehabilitating orangutans is expensive. Caring for orangutans that cannot be rehabilitated is also expensive. Rehab centers often must scramble for funding.

Some conservationists believe rehabilitation could harm wild orangutan populations more than it helps them. They worry that captive orangutans will spread human diseases, such as tuberculosis and hepatitis, to orangutans in the wild. They also point out that some rehabilitated females never learn to be good mothers to their young.

But over the last thirty years, rehab centers have released eight hundred rehabilitated orangutans into the rain forest. Researchers have not found evidence that released orangutans have spread diseases or harmed the wild population.

The Orangutan's Future

Until recently, experts believed about fifteen thousand to twenty-five thousand orangutans remained in the wild, with five thousand to seven thousand in Sumatra and ten thousand to twenty thousand in Borneo. But in the last few years, experts have realized that they had seriously underestimated the wild orangutan population.[2]

In 2002, Nature Conservancy researchers led by scientist Scott Stanley found a previously undiscovered population of orangutans in eastern Borneo. Stanley estimates that two thousand orangutans live in this dense, swampy rain forest.

After forest fires devastated the rain forests of Borneo and Sumatra in the late 1990s, orangutan experts began new studies to find out how many orangutans had survived. In 2004, various wildlife groups combined their data. They found that there are about fifty thousand

▲ *Rehabilitation centers, like this one in Sumatra, provide protection for orangutans that have been displaced, orphaned, or abused. The ultimate goal is to return the apes to the wild.*

orangutans in the wild, nearly twice as many as they had previously thought.

At first, the researchers were reluctant to share their findings, concerned that people would think that orangutans were no longer in danger. They also worried that governments would no longer protect the orangutan as an endangered species, and they were afraid that people would continue to destroy large rain forest areas.

The larger population of orangutans is welcome news. But wildlife experts know that unless humans do everything they can to save orangutans and the rain forest, their habitat, the "wild man of Borneo" could become extinct by the year 2020.

The Endangered and Threatened Wildlife List

This series is based on the Endangered and Threatened Wildlife list compiled by the U.S. Fish and Wildlife Service (USFWS). Each book explores an endangered or threatened animal, tells why it has become endangered or threatened, and explains the efforts being made to restore the species' population.

The United States Fish and Wildlife Service, in the Department of the Interior, and the National Marine Fisheries Service, in the Department of Commerce, share responsibility for administration of the Endangered Species Act.

In 1973, Congress took the farsighted step of creating the Endangered Species Act, widely regarded as the world's strongest and most effective wildlife conservation law. It set an ambitious goal: to reverse the alarming trend of human-caused extinction that threatened the ecosystems we all share.

The complete list of Endangered and Threatened Wildlife and Plants can be found at **http://endangered.fws.gov/wildlife.html#Species**.

Chapter Notes

Chapter 1. The Endangered Orangutan

1. Gary Shapiro, "How Many Orangutans Are There? More Than Last Year . . . But What Does That Mean?" *Orangutan Foundation International,* 2004, <http://www.orangutan.org/projects/howmany2.php> (November 14, 2004).

Chapter 2. Orangutan Characteristics

1. Gisela Kaplan and Lesley J. Rogers, *The Orangutans* (Cambridge, Mass.: Perseus Publishing, 2000), p. 22.

2. Stephen J. O'Brien, *Tears of the Cheetah* (New York: St. Martin's Press, 2003), pp. 128–129.

3. Ibid., p. 129.

4. Ibid., p. 130.

Chapter 4. Orangutan Intelligence

1. Eugene Linden, *The Octopus and the Orangutan: More True Tales of Animal Intrigue, Intelligence, and Ingenuity* (New York: Dutton, 2002), p. 8.

2. Emily Sohn, "An Inspiring Home for Apes," *Science News for Kids,* July 14, 2004, <http://www.sciencenewsforkids.org/articles/20040714/Feature1.asp> (November 14, 2004).

Chapter 5. Saving the Orangutan

1. Lori Perkins, Zoo Atlanta, Chair, Orangutan SSP and International Studbook Keeper for Orangutans, in an interview, January 5, 2004.

2. Gary Shapiro, "How Many Orangutans Are There? More Than Last Year . . . But What Does That Mean?" *Orangutan Foundation International,* 2004, <http://www.orangutan.org/projects/howmany2 .php> (November 14, 2004).

Further Reading

Brend, Stephen. *Orangutan: Habitats, Life Cycles, Food Chains, Threats.* Austin, Tex.: Raintree Steck-Vaughn, 2000.

Galdikas, Biruté M. F., and Nancy Briggs. *Orangutan Odyssey.* New York: Harry N. Abrams, 1999.

Gilders, Michelle A. *The Nature of Great Apes: Our Next of Kin.* New York: Greystone Books, 2000.

Levine, Stuart P. *The Orangutan.* San Diego, Calif.: Lucent Books, 2000.

Linden, Eugene. *The Parrot's Lament and Other True Tales of Animal Intrigue, Intelligence, and Ingenuity.* New York: Dutton, 2002.

Platt, Richard. *Apes and Other Hairy Primates.* London: Dorling Kindersley, 2001.

Ring, Susan. *Project Orangutan.* Mankato, Minn.: Weigl Publishers, 2003.

Russon, Anne E. *Orangutans: Wizards of the Rain Forest.* Toronto: Firefly Books, 2000.

Saign, Geoffrey. *The Great Apes.* New York: Franklin Watts, 1998.

Sloan, Christopher. *The Human Story: Our Evolution From Prehistoric Ancestors to Today.* Washington, D.C.: National Geographic, 2004.

Sourd, Christine. *The Orangutan: Forest Acrobat.* Watertown, Mass.: Charlesbridge Publishing, 2001.

Index

B
babies, 12–13, 14, 22, 24–25, 35, 39, 41
birth, 22–24
bonobos, 16, 20

C
Camp Leakey, 29, 41
Chantek, captive orangutan, 29–30
cheek pads, 15, 19
childhood, 24–25
chimpanzees, 11, 16, 20, 21, 26
CITES, 39
climbing, 17–18, 21
conservation groups, 39–40
culture of orangutans, 30–31

D
diet, 21, 23–24, 37–38

F
food, 21, 23–25, 27
forest fires, 37, 38–39, 43
Fu Mancu, captive orangutan, 29

G
Galdikas, Dr. Biruté, 41, 42
genetics, 16, 20
gorillas, 11, 16, 21, 26
great apes, 11, 16, 20, 22, 26, 31

H
habitat, 10, 11–12, 13–14, 17, 21, 22, 32, 33, 34, 43–44
hair, 10, 15, 17, 19
home range, 23, 25

I
illegal pet trade, 12–14, 39
intelligence, 26–31

L
language, 29–30
logging, 10, 12, 35–37, 38, 39
long call, 19

M
mating, 22

mining, 10, 12, 37–38, 39

N
nests, 24, 25

O
O'Brien, Dr. Stephen J., 20
Orangutan Foundation International, 39, 41–42
Orangutan Language Project, 29

P
Perkins, Lori, 33–34
pet trade, 12–13, 14, 35, 39, 41
physical characteristics, 15, 16–19
plantations, 37, 38, 39
poachers, 12, 14, 35, 39
population, 10, 12, 43–44

R
range, home, 23, 25
rehabilitation centers, 13, 39, 40, 41–43
reproduction, 10, 14, 22, 24–25

S
scientific name, 10, 15, 19
Shapiro, Dr. Gary, 29
sign language, 29–30
size, 10, 13, 17, 18–19
snag ride, 31
species of orangutan, 15, 19–20
Species Survival Plan (SSP), 33, 40
Stanley, Scott, 43
status, 10, 12, 32, 39

T
threats, 10, 12–14, 32–39
throat pouch, 19
tool use, 27–29, 31
tsunami, 14, 32–34

W
walking, 15, 16, 21

Z
Zoo Atlanta, 30, 33, 40–41
zoos, 40–41